Mary,

I'm really glad we're friends. There have been many good times and I hope more to come. Take care of yourself and hopefully I'll see you this summer.

Love Ya Lots!

Happy Graduation!

Love,
Jenni
5/84

P.S. I want a senior picture.

Confessions of a Reluctant Optimist

CONFESSIONS OF A RELUCTANT OPTIMIST

Poems by Phyllis McGinley
Selected by
Barbara Wells Price
Illustrated by
Peter Lippmann

Hallmark Editions

CONFESSIONS
OF A RELUCTANT OPTIMIST

I KNOW A VILLAGE

I know a village facing toward
    Water less sullen than the sea's,
Where flickers get their bed and board
    And all the streets are named for trees.

The streets are named for trees. They edge
    Past random houses, safely fenced
With paling or with privet hedge
    That bicycles can lean against.

And when the roots of maples heave
    The solid pavements up that bound them,
Strollers on sidewalks give them leave
    To thrust, and pick a way around them.

The little boats in harbor wear
    Sails whiter than a summer wedding.
One fountain splashes in a Square.
    In winter there's a hill for sledding;

While through October afternoons
    Horse chestnuts dribble on the grass,
Prized above diamonds or doubloons
    By miser children, shrill from class.

I know a village full of bees
    And gardens lit by canna torches,
Where all the streets are named for trees
    And people visit on their porches.

It looks haphazard to the shore.
    Brown flickers build there. And I'd not
Willing, I think, exchange it for
    Arcadia or Camelot.

SATURDAY STORM

This flooded morning is no time to be
Abroad on any business of mankind.
The rain has lost its casual charity;
It falls and falls and falls and would not mind
Were all the world washed blind.

No creature out of doors goes weatherproof.
Birds cower in their nests. The beast that can
Has found himself a roof.
This hour's for man
To waken late in, putter by his fire,
Leaf through old books or tear old letters up,
Mend household things with bits of thrifty wire,
Refill his coffee cup,
And, thus enclosed in comfort like a shell,
Give thought to, wish them well
Who must this day
On customary errands take their way:

The glistening policemen in the street,
For instance, blowing their whistles
                through the welter
And stamping their wet feet;
And grocery boys flung in and out of shelter
But faithful to their loads;
And people changing tires beside the roads;

Doormen with colds and doctors in damp suits;
And milkmen on their routes,
Scuttling like squirrels; and men with cleated boots
Aloft on telephone poles in the rough gale;
But chiefly trudging men with sacks of mail
Slung over shoulder,
Who slog from door to door and cannot rest
Till they've delivered the last government folder,
The final scribbled postcard, misaddressed.

Oh, all at ease
Should say a prayer for these—
That they come, healthy, homeward before night,
Safer than beasts or birds,
To no dark welcome but an earned delight
Of pleasant words,
Known walls, accustomed love, fires burning steady,
And a good dinner ready.

CONFESSIONS
OF A RELUCTANT OPTIMIST

When flaming comrades I admire
  (And in whose breasts was ever coddled
Dissatisfaction's honest fire)
Argue how to their hearts' desire
  The universe should be remodeled—

When of their wrongs they call the roll,
  Vowing that fortune is a hellion,
Shamefaced I sit, an outcast soul,
  Incapable of true rebellion.

For, though aware that life is what
  One ought to view with wrath and gravity,
I live delighted with my lot,
  Sunk in content as in depravity.

Less woman, I expect, than mouse,
  To alter fate I would not bother.
I like my plain suburban house.
  I like my children and their father.

Quite able to believe the decks
  Are stacked for females—much it boots me!
I would not willing change my sex.
  It is the very sex which suits me.

In fact, I find it hard to see
    Exactly what I ought disparage.
I like my nationality,
    I like my relatives-by-marriage.

Trapped, tricked, enslaved, but lacking sense
    To enter in the conflict single,
I wear my chains like ornaments,
    Convinced they make a charming jingle.

Alas, alack, how well I know
    My kind's a drawback to the nation!
But here I am and here I go,
Contented with the status quo,
    And quite beyond salvation.

RECIPE FOR A MARRIAGE
With a Curtsy to Mr. Burns

John Anderson my jo, John,
    When we were first acquaint,
I had a fault or so, John,
    And you were less than saint.
But once we'd said a brave "I do"
    And paid the parson's fee,
I set about reforming you
    And you reforming me.

John Anderson my jo, John,
    Our years have journeyed fair;
I think, as couples go, John,
    We've made a pleasant pair.
For us, contented man and wife,
    The marriage bond endures,
Since you have changed my way of life
    And I have altered yours.

Let captious people say, John,
    There's poison in that cup.
We found a simple way, John,
    To clear each difference up.
We could not swap our virtues, John,
    So this was our design:
All your bad habits I took on,
    While you adopted mine.

Until the final lightnings strike,
   It's comfortable to know
Our faults we share and share alike,
   John Anderson my jo.

MIDCENTURY LOVE LETTER

Stay near me. Speak my name. Oh, do not wander
By a thought's span, heart's impulse, from the light
We kindle here. You are my sole defender
(As I am yours) in this precipitous night,
Which over earth, till common landmarks alter,
Is falling, without stars, and bitter cold.
We two have but our burning selves for shelter.
Huddle against me. Give me your hand to hold.

So might two climbers lost in mountain weather
On a high slope and taken by the storm,
Desperate in the darkness, cling together
Under one cloak and breathe each other warm.
Stay near me. Spirit, perishable as bone,
In no such winter can survive alone.

ABOUT CHILDREN

By all the published facts in the case,
Children belong to the human race.

Equipped with consciousness, passions, pulse,
They even grow up and become adults.

So why's the resemblance, moral or mental,
Of children to people so coincidental?

Upright out of primordial dens,
Homo walked and was sapiens.

But rare as leviathans or auks
Is—male or female—the child who walks.

He runs, he gallops, he crawls, he pounces,
Flies, leaps, stands on his head, or bounces,

Imitates snakes or the tiger striped
But seldom recalls he is labeled "Biped."

Which man or woman have you set sights on
Who craves to slumber with all the lights on

Yet creeps away to a lampless nook
In order to pore on a comic book?

Why, if (according to A. Gesell)
The minds of children ring clear as a bell,

Does every question one asks a tot
Receive the similar answer—"What?"

And who ever started the baseless rumor
That any child has a sense of humor?

Children conceive of no jest that's madder
Than Daddy falling from a ten-foot ladder.

Their fancies sway like jetsam and flotsam;
One minute they're winsome, the next
       they're swatsome.

While sweet their visages, soft their arts are,
Cold as a mermaiden's kiss their hearts are;

They comprehend neither pity nor treason.
An hour to them is a three months' season.

So who can say—this is just between us—
That children and we are a common genus,

When the selfsame nimbus is eerily worn
By a nymph, a child, and a unicorn?

SMALL-TOWN PARADE
Decoration Day

Below the lawns and picket fences,
　　Just past the firehouse, half a block,
Sharp at eleven-five commences
　　This ardent and memorial walk
　　(Announced, last night, for ten o'clock).

Solemn, beneath the elmy arches,
　　Neighbor and next-door neighbor meet.
For half the village forward marches
　　To the school band's uncertain beat,
　　And half is lined along the street.

O the brave show! O twirling baton!
　　O drummer stepping smartly out!
O mayor, perspiring, with no hat on!
　　O nurses' aid! O martial rout
　　O Bluebird, Brownie, Eagle Scout!

And at the rear, aloof and splendid,
　　Lugging the lanterns of their pride,
O the red firemen, well attended
　　By boys on bicycles who ride
　　With envious reverence at their side!

The morning smells of buds and grasses.
  Birds twitter louder than the flute.
And wives, as the procession passes,
    Wave plodding husbands wild salute
    From porches handy to the route.

Flags snap. And children, vaguely greeted,
  Wander into the ranks a while.
The band, bemused but undefeated,
    Plays Sousa, pedagogic style,
    Clean to the Square—a measured mile.

Until at last by streets grown stony,
  To the gray monument they bring
The wreath which is less testimony
    To Death than Life, continuing
    Through this and every other spring.

THE 5:32

She said, If tomorrow my world were torn in two,
Blacked out, dissolved, I think I would remember
(As if transfixed in unsurrendering amber)
This hour best of all the hours I knew:
When cars came backing into the shabby station,
Children scuffing the seats, and the women driving
With ribbons around their hair,
        and the trains arriving,
And the men getting off with tired
        but practiced motion.

Yes, I would remember my life like this, she said:
Autumn, the platform red with Virginia creeper,
And a man coming toward me, smiling,
        the evening paper
Under his arm, and his hat pushed back on his head;
And wood smoke lying like haze on the quiet town,
And dinner waiting, and the sun not yet gone down.

LAUNCELOT WITH BICYCLE

Her window looks upon the lane.
From it, anonymous and shy,
Twice daily she can see him plain,
Wheeling heroic by.
She droops her cheek against the pane
And gives a little sigh.

Above him maples at their bloom
Shake April pollen down like stars
While he goes whistling past her room
Toward unimagined wars,
A tennis visor for his plume,
Scornful of handlebars.

And, counting over in her mind
His favors, gleaned like windfall fruit
(A morning when he spoke her kind,
An afterschool salute,
A number that she helped him find,
Once, for his paper route),

Sadly she twists a stubby braid
And closer to the casement leans—
A wistful and a lily maid
In moccasins and jeans,
Despairing from the seventh grade
To match his lordly teens.

And so she grieves in Astolat
(Where other girls have grieved the same)
For being young and therefore not
Sufficient to his fame—
Who will by summer have forgot
Grief, April, and his name.

THE TEMPTATIONS
OF SAINT ANTHONY

Off in the wilderness bare and level,
Anthony wrestled with the Devil.
Once he'd beaten the Devil down,
Anthony'd turn his eyes toward town
And leave his hermitage now and then
To come to grips with the souls of men.

Afterward, all the tales agree,
Wrestling the Devil seemed to be
Quite a relief to Anthony.

DANIEL AT BREAKFAST

His paper propped against the electric toaster
    (Nicely adjusted to his morning use),
Daniel at breakfast studies world disaster
    And sips his orange juice.

The words dismay him. Headlines shrilly chatter
    Of famine, storm, death, pestilence, decay.
Daniel is gloomy, reaching for the butter.
    He shudders at the way

War stalks the planet still, and men know hunger,
    Go shelterless, betrayed, may perish soon.
The coffee's weak again. In sudden anger
    Daniel throws down his spoon

And broods a moment on the kitchen faucet
    The plumber mended, but has mended ill;
Recalls tomorrow means a dental visit,
    Laments the grocery bill.

Then, having shifted from his human shoulder
    The universal woe, he drains his cup,
Rebukes the weather (surely turning colder),
    Crumples his napkin up
And, kissing his wife abruptly at the door,
Stamps fiercely off to catch the 8:04.

GOOD HUMOR MAN

Listen! It is the summer's self that ambles
 Through the green lanes with such a coaxing tongue.
Not birds or daisy fields were ever symbols
 More proper to the time than this bell rung
With casual insistence—no, not swallow
 Circling the roof or bee in hollyhock.
His is the season's voice, and children follow,
Panting, from every doorway down the block.

So, long ago, in some such shrill procession
 Perhaps the Hamelin children gave pursuit
To one who wore a red-and-yellow fashion
 Instead of white, but made upon his flute
The selfsame promise plain to every comer:
Unending sweets, imperishable summer.

COLLECTOR'S ITEMS

Some lives are filled with sorrow and woe
    And some with joys ethereal.
But the days may come and the weeks may go,
    My life is filled with cereal.
My cupboards bulge and my shelves are bunchy
With morsels crispy or cracked or crunchy,
With rice things, corn things,
    Barley things, wheaten—
All top-of-the-morn things
    And all uneaten.
Ignored they sparkle, unheard they pop
When once they've yielded the Premium Top.

For Cheerios may be just the fare
    To energize whippersnappers,
But mine consider they've had their share
    As soon as they've filched the wrappers.
Breathes there a child with hopes so dim
That Kix are innocent Kix to him,
Not loot for filling
    His crowded coffers
With Big New Thrilling
    Premium Offers?
If such (as I fervently doubt) there be,
He is no kin to my progeny.

As a gardener lusts for a marigold,
  As a miser loves what he mises,
So dotes the heart of a nine-year-old
  On sending away for prizes.
The postman rings and the mail flies hence
With Premium Tops and fifteen cents.
The postman knocks and the gifts roll in:
Guaranteed cardboard, genuine tin,
Paper gadgets and gadgets plastic,
Things that work till you lose the elastic,
Things to molder in draws and pockets,
Magnets, parachutes, pistols, rockets,
Weapons good for a cop's assistant,
Whistles for dogs that are nonexistent,
Toys designed
  To make mothers tremble,
That fathers find
  They have to assemble,
Things Tom Mixish or Supermanish.
How gadgets come and the box tops vanish!
Then hippity-hop
To the grocer's shop
For a brand-new brand with a Premium Top.

Oh, some lives read like an open book
  And some like a legend hoary.
But life to me, wherever I look,
  Seems one long cereal story.

THE TOM-TOM

This is the day for bicycles.

Yesterday was a swimming day,
    A day for splashing head over heels,
When every child would have screamed dismay
At anything less than dolphin play.
    But today they are all on wheels.
Large and little and middle-sized,
An army of children goes mechanized.
As if for a silver medal,
Around and around they pedal.

And we saw no rockets fly,
    No messenger brought the word.
Yet lonely, lonely, the beaches lie
And the saltiest bathing suit is dry
While every child sweeps breathless by
    Like a bird, like a bird.
How did they know? What sign was sent
To herald the seashore's banishment?
Who proclaimed it the time and weather
For cycling all together?

Tomorrow, or the day after,
    The pedals will lose their power.
Solemn, and yet with laughter,
They will turn to something dafter,
    All at the selfsame hour.
All of a sudden the windy heights
Will burst into gaudy bloom of kites
With a heaven-aspiring reach
And a child attached to each.

But that hour overthrown,
    The falcon kites will be grounded.
As if a bugle had blown,
    As if a signal had sounded,
They will learn as one to be monster tall
When a madness of stilts assails them all.
Together in hot compliance,
They will walk the village like giants.

If you ask them, they are perplext.
    The calendar gives no warning.
One does not tell the next,
    Yet they wake and know in the morning
(As a swallow knows the time
    For quitting a rainy land),
When the rope should whirl to the skipping-rhyme
    Or the baseball thud in the hand,
Or the multitudinous din
Of the roller skates begin.

It is something that tom-toms say.
You cannot explain it away,
    Though reason or judgment reels.
For yesterday was a swimming day
And today is the same as yesterday,
    Yet now they are all on wheels.

ANNIVERSARY

In garden-colored boots he goes
    Ardent around perennial borders
To spray the pink, celestial rose
    Or give a weed its marching orders.

Draining at dawn his hasty cup,
    He takes a train to urban places;
By lamplight, cheerful, figures up
    The cost of camps and dental braces.

And warm upon my shoulders lays
    Impetuous at dinner table
The mantle of familiar praise
    That's better than a coat of sable.

WHAT EVERY WOMAN KNOWS

When little boys are able
    To comprehend the flaws
In their December fable
    And part with Santa Claus,
Although I do not think they grieve,
How burningly they disbelieve!

They cannot wait, they cannot rest
For knowledge nibbling at the breast.
They cannot rest, they cannot wait
To set conniving parents straight.

Branding that comrade as a dunce
Who trusts the saint they trusted once,
With rude guffaw and facial spasm
They publish their iconoclasm,
And find particularly shocking
The thought of hanging up a stocking.

But little girls (no blinder
    When faced by mortal fact)
Are cleverer and kinder
    And brimming full of tact.
The knowingness of little girls
Is hidden underneath their curls.

Obligingly, since parents fancy
The season's tinsel necromancy,
They take some pains to make pretense
Of duped and eager innocence.

Agnostics born but Bernhardts bred,
They hang the stocking by the bed,
Make plans, and pleasure their begetters
By writing Santa lengthy letters,
Only too well aware the fruit
Is shinier plunder, richer loot.

For little boys are rancorous
  When robbed of any myth,
And spiteful and cantankerous
  To all their kin and kith.
But little girls can draw conclusions
And profit from their lost illusions.

A CERTAIN AGE

All of a sudden, bicycles are toys,
Not locomotion. Bicycles are for boys
And seventh-graders, screaming when they talk.
A girl would rather
Take vows, go hungry, put on last year's frock,
Or dance with her own father
Than pedal down the block.

This side of childhood lies a narrow land,
Its laws unwritten, altering out of hand,
But, more than Sparta's, savagely severe.
Common or gentry,
The same taboos prevail. One learns, by ear,
The customs of the country
Or pays her forfeit here.

No bicycles. No outcast dungarees
Over this season's round and scarless knees,
No soft departures from the veering norm.
But the same bangle,
Marked with a nickname, now from every arm
Identically must dangle,
The speech be uniform—

Uniform as the baubles round the throat,
The ill-made wish, the stiffened petticoat,
And beauty, blurred but burning in the face.
Now, scrubbed and scented,
They move together toward some meeting place,
Wearing a regimented,
Unutterable grace.

They travel rapt, each compass pointing south—
Heels to the shoes and lipstick on the mouth.

BALLROOM DANCING CLASS

The little girls' frocks are frilly.
   The little boys' suits are blue.
On little gold chairs
They perch in pairs
   Awaiting their Friday cue.
The little boys stamp like ponies.
   The little girls coo like doves.
The little boys pummel their cronies
   With white, enormous gloves.
And overhead from a balcony
The twittering mothers crane to see.

Though sleek the curls
Of the little girls,
   Tossing their locks like foam,
Each little boy's tie
Has slipped awry
   And his hair forgets the comb.
He harks to the tuning fiddle
   With supercilious sneers.
His voice is cracked in the middle,
   Peculiar are his ears.
And little girls' mothers nod with poise
To distracted mothers of little boys.

Curtsying to the hostess,
    The little girls dip in line.
But hobbledehoy
Bobs each little boy,
    And a ramrod in his spine.
With little girls' charms prevailing,
    Why, as the music starts,
Are the little girls' mothers paling?
    And why do they clasp their hearts
When the hostess says with an arching glance,
"Let boys choose partners before we dance"?

Now little girls sway
Like buds in May
    And tremble upon the stalk.
But little boys wear
An arrogant air
    And they swagger when they walk.
The meagerest boy grows taller.
    The shyest one's done with doubt,
As he fingers a manful collar
    And singles his charmer out,
Or rakes the circle with narrowed eyes
To choose his suitable Friday prize.
While overhead in the balcony
The little boys' mothers smile to see
On razorless cheek and beardless chin
The Lord-of-Creation look begin.

Oh, little boys beckon, little girls bend!
And little boys' mothers condescend
(As they straighten their furs and pat their pearls)
To nod to the mothers of the little girls.

SUNDAY PSALM

This is the day which the Lord hath made,
    Shining like Eden absolved of sin,
Three parts glitter to one part shade:
    Let us be glad and rejoice therein.

Everything's scoured brighter than metal.
    Everything sparkles as pure as glass—
The leaf on the poplar, the zinnia's petal,
    The wing of the bird, and the blade of the grass.

All, all is luster. The glossy harbor
    Dazzles the gulls that, gleaming, fly.
Glimmers the wasp on the grape in the arbor.
    Glisten the clouds in the polished sky.

Tonight—tomorrow—the leaf will fade,
    The waters tarnish, the dark begin.
But *this is the day which the Lord hath made:*
    Let us be glad and rejoice therein.

A GARLAND OF PRECEPTS

Though a seeker since my birth,
Here is all I've learned on earth,
This the gist of what I know:
Give advice and buy a foe.
Random truths are all I find
Stuck like burs about my mind.
Salve a blister. Burn a letter.
Do not wash a cashmere sweater.
Tell a tale but seldom twice.
Give a stone before advice.

Pressed for rules and verities,
All I recollect are these:
Feed a cold to starve a fever.
Argue with no true believer.
Think-too-long is never-act.
Scratch a myth and find a fact.
Stitch in times saves twenty stitches.
Give the rich, to please them, riches.
Give to love your hearth and hall.
But do not give advice at all.

THE ANGRY MAN

The other day I chanced to meet
An angry man upon the street—
A man of wrath, a man of war,
A man who truculently bore
Over his shoulder, like a lance,
A banner labeled "Tolerance."

And when I asked him why he strode
Thus scowling down the human road,
Scowling, he answered, "I am he
Who champions total liberty—
Intolerance being, ma'am, a state
No tolerant man can tolerate.

"When I meet rogues," he cried, "who choose
To cherish oppositional views,
Lady, like this, and in this manner,
I lay about me with my banner
Till they cry mercy, ma'am." His blows
Rained proudly on prospective foes.

Fearful, I turned and left him there
Still muttering, as he thrashed the air,
"Let the Intolerant beware!"

TO A LADY IN A PHONE BOOTH

Plump occupant of Number Eight,
    Outside whose door I shift my parcels
And wait and wait and wait and wait
    With aching nerves and metatarsals,
I long to comprehend the truth:
What keeps you sitting in that booth?

What compact holds you like a stone?
    Whose voice, whose summons rich with power,
Has fixed you to the telephone
    These past three-quarters of an hour?
Can this be love? Or thorns and prickles?
And where do you get all those nickels?

Say, was the roof above you sold
    By nameless landlord, cruel and craven,
Till, driven by imperious cold,
    You find this nook your only haven?
Yield me the instrument you hoard,
And I will share my bed and board.

Perhaps you choose such public place
    To do your lips and change your vesture.
You have not swooned, in any case.
    A motion, an occasional gesture,

Assures me you are safe inside.
You do not sleep. You have not died.

That paper clutched within your fist—
    I cannot quite make out the heading—
Madam, is that a formal list?
    Do you, by chance, arrange a wedding?
Or—dreadful thought I dare not speak!—
Perhaps you rent here by the week.

Well, likely I shall never know.
    My arches fall, my patience ravels.
And with these bundles I must go,
    Frustrated, forth upon my travels.
Behind the unrevealing pane
The mystery and you remain.

Yet, as I totter out of line,
    A faint suspicion waxes stronger.
Oh, could it be your feet, like mine,
    Would simply bear you up no longer?
So did you happen, unaware,
Upon this cubicle, with chair,

And did it seem in all the town
One spot where you could just sit down?

JUNE IN THE SUBURBS

Not with a whimper but a roar
Of birth and bloom this month commences.
The wren's a gossip at her door.
Roses explode along the fences.

By day the chattering mowers cope
With grass decreed a final winner.
Darkness delays. The skipping rope
Twirls in the driveway after dinner.

Through lupine-lighted borders now
For winter bones Dalmatians forage.
Costly, the spray on apple bough.
The canvas chair comes out of storage;

And rose-red golfers dream of par,
And class-bound children loathe their labors,
While pilgrims, touring gardens, are
Cold to petunias of their neighbors.

Now from damp loafers nightly spills
The sand. Brides lodge their lists with Plummer.
And cooks devise on charcoal grills
The first burnt offerings of summer.

INCIDENT IN THE AFTERNOON

I heard two ladies at a play—
    A comedy considered witty.
It was a Wednesday matinée
    And they had come from Garden City.
Their frocks were rather arts-and-crafts,
And they had lunched, I learned, at Schrafft's.

Although we did not speak or bow
    Or comment even on the weather,
More intimate I know them now
    Than if we'd gone to school together.
(As you must presently divine,
Their seats were rather near to mine.)

Before the curtain rose I heard
    What each had told her spouse that morning.
I learned the history, word for word,
    Of why three cooks had given warning.
Also that neither cared a straw
For domineering sons-in-law.

I heard a bridge hand, play by play.
    I heard how all's not gold that glitters.
I heard a moral résumé
    Of half a dozen baby-sitters.

I learned beyond the slightest question
Shrimps are a trial to digestion.

The lights went down. The stage was set.
    Still, in the dusk that fans the senses,
Those ladies I had never met
    Poured out their swollen confidences.
The dialogue was smart. It stirred them
To conversation. And I heard them.

Above each stylish epigram
    Wherewith the hero mocked his rival,
They proved how nicely curried lamb
    Might justify a roast's revival,
That some best-selling author's recent
Book was lively. But indecent.

I heard a list of maladies
    Their all too solid flesh was heir to.
I heard that one, in her deep freeze,
    Could store a steer, but did not care to.
A neighbor's delicate condition
I heard of, all through intermission.

They laid their lives, like open tomes,
    Upon my lap and turned the pages.
I heard their taste in hats and homes,
    Their politics, but not their ages.

So much I heard of strange and true
Almost it reconciled me to
One fact, unseemly to recall:
I did not hear the play at all.

EPITAPHS FOR
THREE PROMINENT PERSONS

The Independent
So open was his mind, so wide
To welcome winds from every side
That public weather took dominion,
Sweeping him bare of all opinion.

The Statesman
He did not fear his enemies
    Nor their despiteful ends,
But not the seraphs on their knees
    Could save him from his friends.

The Demagogue
That trumpet tongue which taught a nation
Loud lessons in vituperation
Teaches it yet another, viz:
How sweet the noise of silence is.

REACTIONARY ESSAY
ON APPLIED SCIENCE

I cannot love the Brothers Wright.
 Marconi wins my mixed devotion.
 Had no one yet discovered Flight
 Or set the air waves in commotion,
Life would, I think, have been as well.
That also goes for A. G. Bell.

What I'm really thankful for,
 when I'm cleaning up after lunch,
Is the invention of waxed paper.

That Edison improved my lot,
 I sometimes doubt; nor care a jitney
Whether the kettle steamed, or Watt,
 Or if the gin invented Whitney.
Better the world, I often feel,
Had nobody contrived the wheel.

On the other hand, I'm awfully indebted
To whoever it was dreamed up the elastic band.

Yes, pausing grateful, now and then,
 Upon my prim, domestic courses,
I offer praise to lesser men—
 Fultons unsung, anonymous Morses—

Whose deft and innocent devices
Pleasure my house with sweets and spices.

I give you, for instance, the fellow
Who first had the idea for Scotch Tape.

I hail the man who thought of soap,
    The chap responsible for zippers,
Sun lotion, the stamped envelope,
    And screens, and wading pools for nippers,
Venetian blinds of various classes,
And bobby pins and tinted glasses.

DeForest never thought up anything
So useful as a bobby pin.

Those baubles are the ones that keep
    Their places, and beget no trouble,
Incite no battles, stab no sleep,
    Reduce no villages to rubble,
Being primarily designed
By men of unambitious mind.

You remember how Orville Wright said
    his flying machine
Was going to outlaw war?

Let them on Archimedes dote
　　Who like to hear the planet rattling.
I cannot cast a hearty vote
　　For Galileo or for Gatling,
Preferring, of the Freaks of science,
The pygmies rather than the giants—

*(And from experience being wary of
Greek geniuses bearing gifts)*—

Deciding, on reflection calm,
　　Mankind is better off with trifles:
With Band-Aid rather than the bomb,
　　With safety match than safety rifles.
Let the earth fall or the earth spin!
A brave new world might well begin
With no invention
Worth the mention
Save paper towels and aspirin.

*Remind me to call the repairman
About my big, new,
　　automatically defrosting refrigerator
　　with the built-in electric eye.*

CHRISTMAS EVE
IN OUR VILLAGE

Main Street is gay. Each lamppost glimmers,
    Crowned with a blue, electric star.
The gift tree by our fountain shimmers,
    Superbly tall, if angular
    (Donated by the Men's Bazaar).

With garlands proper to the times
    Our doors are wreathed, our lintels strewn.
From our two steeples sound the chimes,
    Incessant, through the afternoon,
    Only a little out of tune.

Breathless with boxes hard to handle,
    The grocery drivers come and go.
Madam the Chairman lights a candle
    To introduce our club's tableau.
    The hopeful children pray for snow.

They cluster, mittened, in the park
    To talk of morning, half affrighted,
And early comes the winter dark
    And early are our windows lighted
    To wheedle homeward the benighted.

The eggnog's lifted for libation,
    Silent at last the postman's ring,
But on the plaza near the station
    The carolers are caroling.

"O Little Town!" the carolers sing.

THIS SIDE OF CALVIN

The Reverend Dr. Harcourt, folk agree,
    Nodding their heads in solid satisfaction,
Is just the man for this community.
    Tall, young, urbane, but capable of action,
He pleases where he serves. He marshals out
    The younger crowd, lacks trace of clerical unction,
Cheers the Kiwanis and the Eagle Scout,
    Is popular at every public function.

And in the pulpit eloquently speaks
    On divers matters with both wit and clarity.
Art, Education, God, the Early Greeks,
    Psychiatry, Saint Paul, true Christian charity,
Vestry repairs that shortly must begin,
    All things but Sin. He seldom mentions Sin.

THE DAY AFTER SUNDAY

Always on Monday, God's in the morning papers,
 His Name is a headline, His Works
   are rumored abroad.
Having been praised by men who are movers
   and shapers,
 From prominent Sunday pulpits,
   newsworthy is God.

On page 27, just opposite Fashion Trends,
 One reads at a glance how He scolded the Baptists
   a little,
Was firm with the Catholics,
   practical with the Friends,
 To Unitarians pleasantly noncommittal.

In print are His numerous aspects, too: God smiling,
 God vexed, God thunderous, God whose mansions
   are pearl,
Political God, God frugal, God reconciling
 Himself with science, God guiding
   the Camp Fire Girl.

Always on Monday morning the press reports
 God as revealed to His vicars in various guises—
Benevolent, stormy, patient, or out of sorts.
 God knows which God is the God God recognizes.

SOLDIER ASLEEP

Soldier asleep, and stirring in your sleep,
In tent, trench, dugout, foxhole, or swampy slough,
I pray the Lord your rifle and soul to keep,
And your body, too,

From the hid sniper in the leafy tangle,
From shrapnel, from the barbed and merciless wire,
From tank, from bomb, from the booby trap
        in the jungle,
From water, from fire.

It was an evil wind that blew you hither,
Soldier, to this strange bed—
A tempest brewed from the world's
        malignant weather.

Safe may you sleep, instead,
Once more in the room with the pennants
        tacked on the wall,
Or the room in the bachelor apartment, 17 L,
The club room, the furnished room across the hall,
The room in the cheap hotel,

The double-decker at home, the bench in the park,
The attic cot, the hammock under the willow,
Or the wide bed in the remembered dark
With the belovèd's head beside you on the pillow.

Safe may the winds return you to the place
That, howsoever it was, was better than this.

LANDSCAPE WITHOUT FIGURES

The shape of the summer has not changed at all.
  There is no difference in the sky's rich color,
In texture of cloud or leaf or languid hill.
  The fringed wave is no duller.

Even the look of this village does not change—
  Shady and full of gardens and near the sea.
But something is lacking. Something sad
        and strange
  Troubles the memory.

Where are they?—the boys, not children
        and not men,
  In polo shirts or jeans or autographed blazers,
With voices suddenly deep, and proud on each chin
  The mark of new razors.

They were workers or players, but always
        the town was theirs.
  They wiped your windshield, they manned
        the parking lots.
They delivered your groceries. They drove
        incredible cars
  As if they were chariots.

They were the lifeguards, self-conscious,
        with little whistles.
    They owned the tennis courts
        and the Saturday dances.
They were barbarous-dark with sun. They were vain
        of their muscles
    And the girls' glances.

They boasted, and swam, and lounged
        at the drugstore's portal.
    They sailed their boats and carried
        new records down.
They never took thought but that they were
        immortal,
    And neither did the town.

But now they are gone like leaves, like leaves
        in the fall,
Though the shape of the summer
        has not changed at all.

from GREETING CARD
FOR BIBLIOPHILES

Readers of essay or continued story;
You who delight in large print or in small;
You constant readers and you desultory;
Readers in bed; readers in easy chairs
With esoteric tomes upon your laps;
Desk-readers; you who read in middle-air,
Hanging from subway straps;
Readers who munch
A chapter with your lunch
Or only read on evenings when it rains;
Readers on trains;
All you who browse in bookshops, at your clubs,
Or, indolent, in tubs;
Who plump for Plutarch or who love a sequel—
I send you greetings warm and free and equal.

Blessings and little sorrow
On you that lend books; yes, and you that borrow;
All readers, whether stirred
By Aristophanes or comic strip;
You dogged ones that finish every word;
And you that skip;
The margin-scribblers and the question-noters;
Quoters;
Readers of any style,
Young, aging, juvenile.
I wish you well, I wish you very well.

*Set at the Rochester Typographic Service, Inc.,
in Caslon Old Face, designed by William Caslon
about 1725. This English typeface was based on
seventeenth-century Dutch designs.
Printed on Hallmark Eggshell Book paper.
Designed by Rainer K. Koenig.*